FEB 0 9 2017

P9-DMS-428

HOW-TO LIBRARY

MAKING KNOT PROJECTS

By Dana Meachen Rau • Illustrated by Kathleen Petelinsek

CHERRY LAKE PUBLISHING • ANN ARBOR, MICHIGAN

CHERRY
LAKE
Publishing

Published in the United States of America by Cherry Lake Publishing
Ann Arbor, Michigan
www.cherrylakepublishing.com

Photo Credits: Page 4, ©lzf/Shutterstock; page 5, ©Brent Hofacker/Shutterstock; page 6, ©Jutawan Diloksambandh/Shutterstock; page 7, ©Lapina/Shutterstock; page 9, ©The Red-E/Shutterstock; page 13, ©Sergey Mironov/Shutterstock; page 29, ©Jeffrey B. Banke/Shutterstock; page 32, ©Charlie Rau.

Library of Congress Cataloging-in-Publication Data
Names: Rau, Dana Meachen, 1971– author.
Title: Making knot projects / by Dana Meachen Rau.
Description: Ann Arbor, Michigan : Cherry Lake Publishing, [2016] |
    Series: How-to library. Crafts | Audience: Grades 4 to 6. | Includes
    bibliographical references and index.
Identifiers: LCCN 2016001611 | ISBN 9781634714204 (lib. bdg.) |
    ISBN 9781634714365 (pbk.) | ISBN 9781634714280 (pdf) |
    ISBN 9781634714440 (ebook)
Subjects: LCSH: Macrambe—Juvenile literature. | Knots and splices—
    Juvenile literature. | Handicraft--Juvenile literature.
Classification: LCC TT840.M33 R38 2016 | DDC 746.42/2—dc23
LC record available at http://lccn.loc.gov/2016001611

Cherry Lake Publishing would like to acknowledge the work of the Partnership for 21st Century Learning. Please visit www.p21.org for more information.

Printed in the United States of America
Corporate Graphics
July 2016

HOW-TO LIBRARY

TABLE OF CONTENTS

Why Knot?

You make a knot every time you tie your shoe.

Knots are very useful. Boaters and fishermen use knots to tie down sails or pull in lobsters. Rock climbers use knots to keep themselves safe while climbing. Search-and-rescue teams know all sorts of helpful knots. So do campers, soldiers, and farmers. Knitters and crocheters use knots to make sweaters and blankets. Doctors use knots to make stitches.

You probably tie knots every day. Need proof? Look at your shoes. A handy knot probably holds your laces in place! If you are a Boy Scout or Girl Scout, you may also have learned how to make many other types of knots.

Knots can also be decorative. You can use them to make jewelry, belts, key chains, and even works of art. So try some of the knotting activities in this book. Why knot? It's fun!

A pretzel is a tasty sort of knot!

Knot History

Nets are made by knotting ropes together.

Knots have probably been around for as long as people have needed to lift, pull, or attach things. Ancient people used knots to make tools such as arrows, **snares**, and nets to catch animals for food. They used knots to pull stones for large building projects such as the pyramids in Egypt.

Ancient knots were both **practical** and artistic. Sailors used knots to tie down sails and make hammocks. In South America, the Incas knotted cords called quipus to keep track of important numbers and other information. Chinese knots and Celtic knots are beautiful works of art.

Many **textile** arts involve knots. Knitting is a way of making knots on two long needles. Crocheting creates knots using a hook. Macramé is an art form combining simple knots to make amazing creations.

You can make some amazing knot creations of your own!

Crafting techniques such as crochet and knitting use knots to turn yarn into blankets, sweaters, and other useful objects.

Basic Supplies

You don't need many supplies to make knots. The most important thing you'll need is plenty of cord.

Types of Cord

- Embroidery floss is made of thin, gathered strands of thread. It is inexpensive and comes in every color you can imagine. This type of cord is best for making friendship bracelets.
- Paracord is a lightweight nylon cord used for parachute lines. Its smooth surface is easy to tie and creates a nice look for decorative projects.
- Hemp cord has a rough, natural look. You can buy it in its natural brown color or dyed in other colors.

You can find these cords—as well as many other types made of silk, leather, cotton, plastic, and elastic—at craft and sewing stores.

Embroidery floss

Paracord

Hemp cord

Other Supplies

A knotting board is made up of a piece of cardboard that is about the size of a notebook, and a binder clip. The board provides a flat work surface, and the clip holds your work in place.

You will also need scissors for cutting cord, a tape measure for measuring it, and a straight pin to help you take out knots if you make a mistake.

If you're making bracelets and belts, you will need clasps to hold them on. Clasps can be found in the jewelry or beading sections of craft stores. They come in many types, such as spring rings, lobster claws, magnetic clasps, D-rings, and slide-release buckles.

For some of the projects in this book, you will need index cards, beads, and sticks. It's also helpful to keep a pencil and paper handy to sketch ideas, draw patterns, or keep track of rows.

SAFETY TIP

Paracord unravels when you cut it. The ends need to be burned with matches or a lighter so they melt and form a seal. Do not use matches yourself. Ask an adult to help with this part of the paracord bracelet project (see page 24).

Basic Knots and Ends

Tying the Knots

Larks Head Knot

1. You will need one cord. Fold it in half to make a loop.
2. Place the loop over the top of a rod or some other object.
3. Thread the loose ends through the loop and pull tight.

Overhand Knot

1. Make a loop so that the working end lays over the rest of the cord. The working end is the end of the cord that you are tying into knots.
2. Tuck the working end into the loop from back to front. Pull on both ends to tighten.

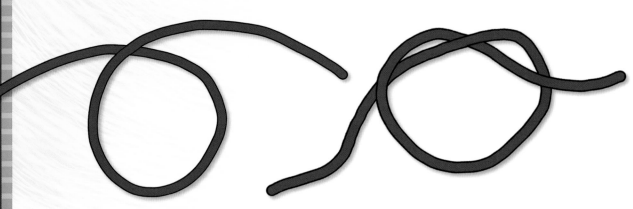

Half Hitch Knot

1. You will need two cords. One cord is the base cord. The other is the tying cord.

2. Place the tying cord over the base cord to form a loop. If you want to work toward the right, the loop needs to be on the left side of the base cord. If you want to work toward the left, the loop needs to be on the right side of the base cord.

3. Tuck the working end of the tying cord under the base cord and up through the loop.

4. Holding the base cord **taut**, pull on the tying cord so that the knot you've created travels up the base cord to the top. This is a single half hitch. The nub you've created should be the color of the tying cord. If it isn't, you may not have held the base cord tight enough.

5. Repeat steps 2 and 3. You now have a double half hitch knot.

Square Knot

1. You will need four cords. The two center cords are the base cords. The two outer cords are the tying cords.

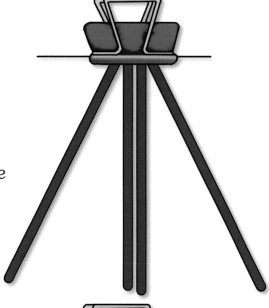

2. Place the left tying cord over the base cords to make a loop on the left side. Place the right tying cord over the left tying cord.

3. Tuck the working end of the right tying cord under the base cords and up through the loop. Pull tightly on both tying cords. You now have a half knot.

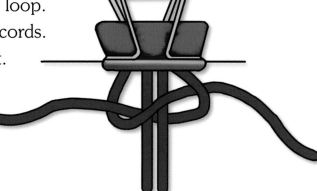

4. Place the left tying cord under the base cords to make a loop on the left side. Place the right tying cord under the left tying cord.

5. Tuck the working end of the right tying cord over the base cords and down through the loop.

6. Pull tightly on both tying cords. You now have a square knot.

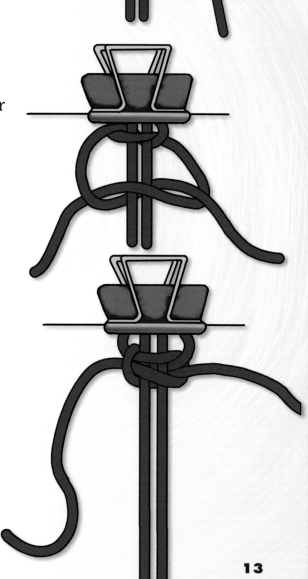

Tying the Ends

There are a few different ways to end a knot project, especially for bracelets.

Tie the ends together

- You can tie the ends of the cords with two overhand knots around your wrist. Trim off the excess cord. This is best for a bracelet that you don't need to take off.

- You can start with a loop at the beginning of your bracelet. When you reach the end, separate the strands into two sections and knot them together. Trim off the excess cord. Loosely tie and untie these strands around the loop to put on and take off your bracelet.

- You can add a metal clasp. Clasps have two parts: a ring and the clasp. Connect the ring to the strands at the beginning of your bracelet with a larks head knot. Use an overhand knot to attach the strands at the end to the clasp. Trim off any excess cord.

A metal clasp and ring connect this bracelet.

Measuring Tips

When working with embroidery floss:
To make a six- or eight-strand bracelet, you will need floss that is about six times as long as your wrist measurement. For example, if your wrist measures 7 inches (17.8 centimeters), multiply that number by six. Each tying cord will need to be 42 inches long (106.7 cm). If you are going to have a loop or larks head knot at the beginning of the project, double the measurement for each color of floss. For example, for a 7-inch (17.8 cm) wrist, the floss should be 84 inches (213.4 cm) long.

When working with paracord:
You will need cord that is about 12 times as long as your wrist measurement. For example, if your wrist measures 6 inches (15.2 cm), you will need about 72 inches (182.9 cm) of paracord.

For all types of cord, always add a little extra so you don't run out as you work. If you do run out of cord by mistake, connect a new piece to the old with an overhand knot (see page 10). Just make sure the knot ends up in the back.

Braid Bracelets

Braiding isn't just for hair. You can braid cords to make interesting patterns on bracelets, too. Decide how you will clasp or tie your bracelet (see page 14) so you can start and end your project as needed.

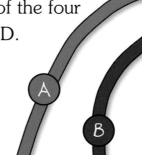

Three-Strand Bracelet

You will need three cords of the same length.

1. Cross the left strand over the middle strand.
2. Cross the right strand over the new middle strand.
3. Continue crossing the outside strands over the middle strand, **alternating** left and right until you reach the end.

Four-Strand Bracelet

You will need two cords of the same length.

1. Loop the middle of one cord over the middle of the other. Think of the four loose ends as A, B, C, and D.

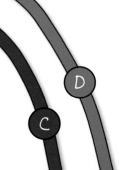

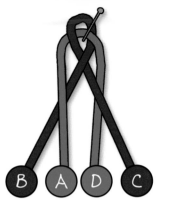
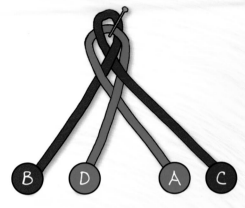

2. Cross A over B and C over D.

3. Cross D over A. Pull on all the cords to tighten.

4. Think of the loose ends from left to right as A, B, C, and D again. Repeat steps 2 and 3 until you reach the end.

Seesaw Bracelet

You will need two cords of the same length.

1. Tie a single half hitch knot with the left cord as the tying cord and the right cord as the base cord (see page 11).

2. Tie a single half hitch knot with the right cord as the tying cord and the left cord as the base cord.

3. Continue alternating single half hitch knots on the left and right cords until you reach the end.

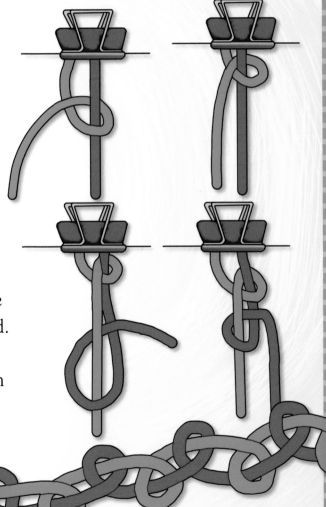

Rainbow Friendship Bracelet

Use all the colors of the rainbow to make a cheery bracelet you can share with someone you care about.

Materials

- Embroidery floss in red, orange, yellow, green, blue, and purple
- Tape measure
- Scissors
- Knotting board

Steps

1. Cut the needed length of floss from each color (see measuring tips on page 15). Gather the ends and tie them in a loose overhand knot, leaving about a 6-inch (15.2 cm) tail.
2. Clip the strands to your knotting board above the knot. Arrange them in the order they would be on a rainbow: red, orange, yellow, green, blue, purple.

3. Start on the left. You will be moving toward the right. Red will be your tying cord. Orange will be your base cord. Tie a double half hitch knot (see page 11).

4. Red will be your tying cord again. But this time, yellow will be your base cord. Tie a double half hitch knot. Continue tying double half hitch knots with the red tying cord across the green, blue, and purple cords. When you finish, the red strand will be on the right. You have completed a row.

5. Repeat steps 3 and 4 with orange as your tying cord. Then repeat with yellow, green, blue, and purple. Once you have worked all the colors as tying cords, you will have a set of rainbow-colored stripes.

6. Continue making full sets of rainbow stripes until your bracelet is the right length. Take the bracelet off the board. Untie the top overhand knot, then tie the bracelet ends together on your wrist.

As the bracelet grows longer, you can unclip it from the board, move it up, and clip it again. This will make it easier to work.

Chevron
Friendship Bracelet

A chevron pattern is made up of V shapes. You will only need four colors for this bracelet, but you will be working with eight strands. Decide how you will clasp or tie your bracelet (see page 14) so you can start and end the project as needed.

Materials
- Embroidery floss in four colors
- Tape measure
- Scissors
- Knotting board

Steps
1. Cut the needed length of floss from each color (see measuring tips on page 15). Gather your strands and fold them at the center. Tie them in a tight overhand knot to form a loop, or attach them to the ring of a clasp.
2. Clip your project to your board. Arrange the strands so their colors are **symmetrical**. You can think of them as colors A1, B1, C1, D1, D2, C2, B2, and A2.

A1 A2
B1 B2
C1 C2
D1 D2

3. Starting on the left, tie color A1 toward the right in double half hitch knots across base cords B1, C1, and D1.

4. Starting on the right, tie color A2 toward the left in double half hitch knots across base cords B2, C2, and D2.

5. Color A1 and A2 are now in the center. Double half hitch knot these strands together. You have completed one row.

6. Tie colors B1 and B2 from both sides into the center. Then continue with C and D to complete a full set of colors. Repeat the pattern until your bracelet is the right length.

Knot the ends or tie on a clasp.

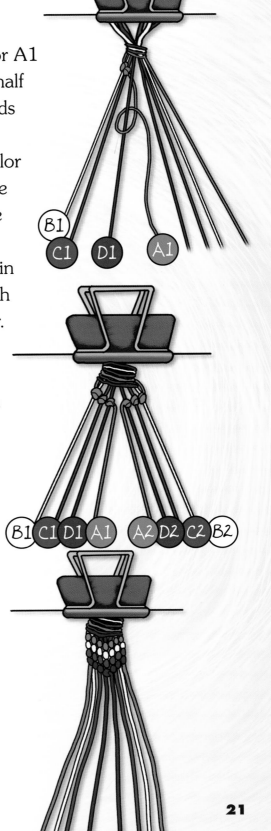

Striped Yarn Belt

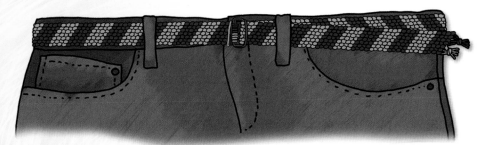

You can use double half hitch knots for more than just friendship bracelets. By using thicker cords, such as yarn, you can make a colorful belt. Choose your two favorite colors to make this striped fashion **accessory**.

Materials

- Two 35-foot (10.7 meters) lengths of medium-weight yarn in color A
- Two 35-foot (10.7 m) lengths of medium-weight yarn in color B
- Two D-rings
- Knotting board
- Tape measure
- Scissors

Steps

1. Gather your strands and fold them at the center. Attach them to both D-rings with a larks head knot.
2. Clip the D-rings to your board. Arrange the cords as A1, A2, A3, A4, B1, B2, B3, and B4.

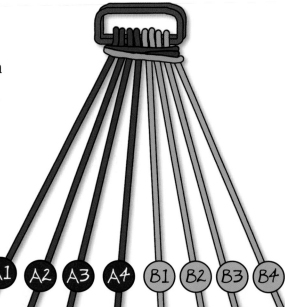

3. Starting with color A1 on the left, tie double half hitch knots toward the right across all the base cords as you would for the rainbow friendship bracelet project (see pages 18 to 19). Continue with cords A2, A3, A4, B1, B2, B3, and B4. You'll see the striped pattern start to form.

4. Continue tying until the belt is the length of your waist measurement plus about 8 inches (20.3 cm). Separate the color A and color B cords. Tie the four strands of each color in an overhand knot. Trim off the excess yarn, leaving some on the end as **fringe**.

5. To wear the belt, stick the end through both rings. Then thread the end back through one ring. Pull to tighten.

You will be working with very long lengths of yarn in this project. To keep the strands from tangling together, it is helpful to make **bobbins** before you start.

1. Fold an index card in half, then fold it in half again. Cut two slits into the folded edge, one near each end.

2. Slip the end of the yarn into one of the slits. Wrap the yarn around and around the card. Slip the yarn into the other slit to hold it in place.

3. Let out the yarn bit by bit as you work.

Paracord Survival Bracelet

Soldiers and campers sometimes wear survival bracelets. If they need cord on their travels, all they have to do is unravel their bracelets. But don't worry—you don't have to unravel this bracelet if you don't want to!

Materials

- About 10 feet (3 m) of paracord
- Slide-release buckle
- Knotting board
- Tape measure
- Fabric scissors
- Matches

Steps

1. Slip both ends of the paracord into one half of the slide-release buckle from back to front and pull them almost all of the way through. Tie a larks head knot.
2. Slip the ends into the other half of the buckle from front to back. Pull the cords through until the length between buckles is about the size of your wrist.

3. Attach the buckles together on your wrist to get a more **accurate** measurement. Pull on the loose ends until the bracelet fits well. You don't want it to be too tight or too loose. Make sure you can still slip two fingers between the buckle and your wrist.

4. Carefully take off the bracelet so you don't lose your measurement. Clip the unknotted buckle end to the top of your board. You should have four strands hanging down. The middle two are tied to the other half of the buckle. The other two are loose.

5. Tie the outer tying cords onto the base cords with a square knot (see pages 12 to 13). Be sure to pull the ends tight.

6. Continue tying square knots until you reach the end. Do not tighten the last knot.

7. Flip your bracelet over so the back side is showing. Tuck the two working ends into the last two stitches. Pull everything tight.

8. Use the fabric scissors to trim the ends. Ask an adult to burn the ends to keep them from unraveling. Do not try to do this part of the project yourself!

9. To wear your bracelet, simply clip it onto your wrist.

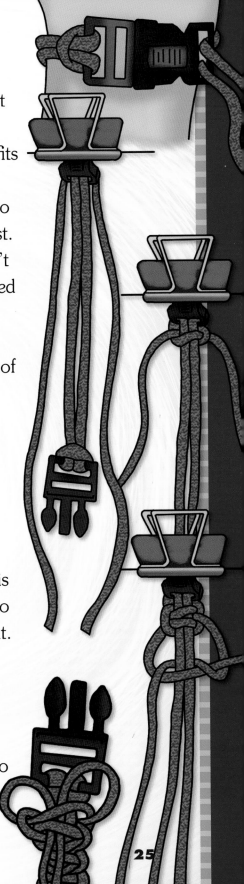

Beaded Wall Hanging

Dress up your walls with a beautiful pattern made of alternating square knots and beads. Sticks, hemp cord, and wooden beads give this project a natural look.

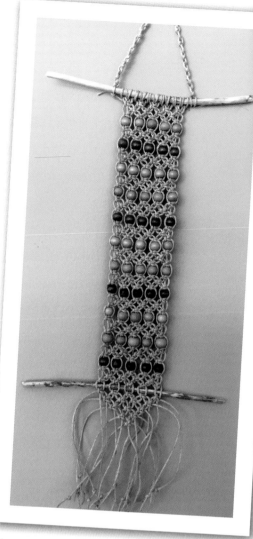

Materials

- Ten 9-foot (2.7 m) lengths of hemp cord
- Two 6-inch (15.2 cm) sticks
- Knotting board
- Wooden beads
- Tape measure
- Scissors
- One 3-foot (0.9 m) length of hemp cord

Steps

1. Fold each of the 9-foot (2.7 m) cords in half. Tie them to one of the sticks using larks head knots. Attach the stick to your board with clips.
2. Use the first four cords to tie a square knot (see pages 12 to 13). The second and third strands will be base cords.

A close-up showing how to start step three

The first and fourth strands will be tying cords. Continue across all the sets of cords. You will have a row with five square knots.

3. For the next row, you will connect these five sets together with square knots. Starting on the left, use the right tying cord of the first set and the left tying cord of the second set as base cords. Tie a square knot. Continue this across the other sets. You will now have a row with four square knots.

4. Repeat step 2 to make another row with five square knots.

5. Thread a wooden bead onto each set of base cords. Tie a square knot under each bead to hold it in place.

6. Repeat steps 3 to 5—a row of four square knots, a row of five square knots, a row of beads, and a row of five square knots. Continue in this way until your project is the right length.

27

7. For the next row, place the base cords in front of the other stick and the tying cords behind it. Tie square knots below the stick across the five sets to hold the stick in place.

8. For the next row, tie four alternating square knots.

9. For the next row, tie three square knots, then two, and finally just one. You will have created a triangle shape.

10. Trim the ends to about 4 inches (10.2 cm) long. Secure each end with an overhand knot.

11. To hang your project, fold the 3-foot (0.9 m) length of cord in half. Attach it to one end of the top stick using a larks head knot. Tie the cord with a seesaw pattern (see page 17) until you reach the right length. Tie the loose ends to the other side of the stick with two overhand knots. Trim any excess cord.

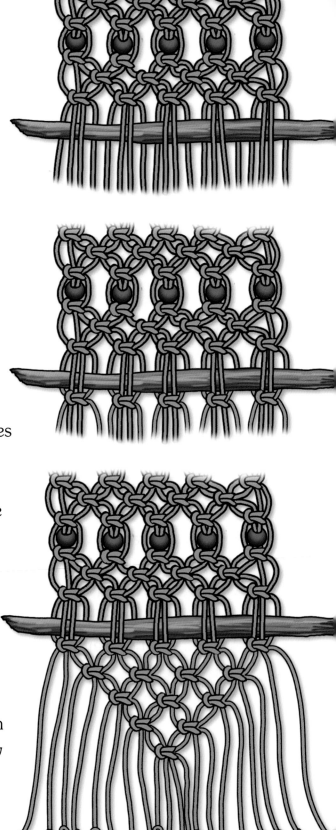

Mix and Match Ideas

You've learned a lot of different knot skills while making the projects in this book. Now it's time to experiment! Mix and match different cords, knots, and clasps. Here are some ideas:

- Follow the steps for the paracord bracelet on pages 24 to 25, but make it longer to use as a dog collar, a belt, or even a leash.
- Instead of attaching friendship bracelets to jewelry clasps, attach them to key rings to make unique handcrafted key chains.
- If you don't like the natural look of the wall hanging on page 26, jazz it up by using colorful party straws instead of sticks, silk cord instead of hemp, and plastic pony beads instead of wooden ones.
- Try the braided bracelet techniques on pages 16 to 17 in your hair!

Think small. Think big. Think any way you want to create decorative and useful crafts with knots.

Knots look great on many accessories!

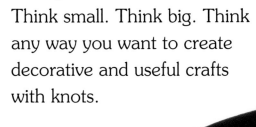

Glossary

accessory (ak-SES-ur-ee) a small item such as a piece of jewelry, a belt, or a bag that is worn with clothes

accurate (AK-yuh-rit) correct and exact

alternating (AWL-tur-nay-ting) going back and forth between two things

bobbins (BAH-binz) devices used to hold thread

fringe (FRINJ) loose threads at the edge of an item of clothing

practical (PRAK-ti-kuhl) useful and sensible

snares (SNAIRZ) loops of wire or cord that are used to capture animals

symmetrical (si-MET-ri-kuhl) exactly the same on both sides of a center line

taut (TAWT) stretched tight

textile (TEK-stile) woven or knitted fabric or cloth

For More Information

Books

Pshednovek, Ariela. *Spectacular Friendship Bracelets*. Watertown, MA: Charlesbridge, 2016.

Stetson, Emily. 40 *Knots to Know: Hitches, Loops, Bends and Bindings.* Charlotte, VT: Williamson Publishing Company, 2002.

Strutt, Laura. *Arm Candy: Friendship Bracelets to Make and Share.* Hauppauge, NY: Barron's Educational Series, Inc., 2015.

Sundsten, Berndt, and Jan Jäger. *My First Book of Knots*. New York: Skyhorse, 2009.

Web Sites

Animated Knots by Grog

www.animatedknots.com

This site is filled with videos to show you how to tie all sorts of knots.

Instructables: Knots!

www.instructables.com/id/Knots

Check out instructions for all kinds of knot projects.

Index

About the Author

Dana Meachen Rau is the author of more than
300 books for children on many topics, including
science, history, cooking, and crafts. She creates,
experiments, researches, and writes from her home
office in Burlington, Connecticut.